BEST OF
Grover Washington, Jr.

Photo by Brahm Schatia

Transcribed by David Pearl

Cover photo by Jeff Sedik
www.jazzandbluesmasters.com

ISBN 978-1-57560-490-9

Visit our website at www.cherrylane.com

Grover Washington, Jr.

Grover Washington's love of music began when he was a child growing up in Buffalo, New York, where his mother (who sang in church choirs) and father (a collector of jazz 78s and an amateur saxophonist) bought him a saxophone at age ten. His passion for supporting individual expression explains why Washington had been involved in such programs as Harman International's "Harman: How to Listen" tour as a music educator for young people and the National Academy of Recording Arts and Sciences (NARAS) education program "Grammy in the Schools" as an instructor, and why he'd conducted seminars and master classes at all grade levels on a continuing basis.

"After I started playing," Washington said, "I'd sneak into clubs to watch guys like Jack McDuff, Harold Vick, and Charles Lloyd. My professional life began at age 12. I played a lot of R & B, blues, and what we used to call 'gut-bucket.'"

Even though he'd studied classical music, Washington's first love was always jazz. "I still listen to the 'classics,'" he said. "Coleman Hawkins, Ben Webster, Don Byas, Lester Young, Charlie Parker, John Coltrane—they're the masters. They will always be relevant. What I strive for in my music is always to tell a story, to portray my inner feelings, like those players."

Washington was doing just that by age 16. After graduating high school, he left Buffalo to play in the Midwest with friends in a group called Four Clefs. "I found myself playing piano one night, saxophone the next, bass the following night," he remembered. Soon afterward, he was drafted into the army. During that time, he made some important connections. A fellow army band member, drummer Billy Cobham, introduced him to several prominent New York musicians, and Washington soon began freelancing in New York and Philadelphia. He met his wife in Philadelphia in 1966 while stationed at Fort Dix, NJ, in the 19th Army Band.

After playing for organist Charles Earland and recording as a sideman for the CTI and Prestige labels, Washington recorded *Breakout* with Johnny "Hammond" Smith. The album was a bestseller and established Washington as a major new voice on saxophone. His big break came in 1970, when Hank Crawford couldn't make a session. Creed Taylor turned the date over to Washington, who'd been playing in the horn section for the session. The result was *Inner City Blues,* released in 1971, while Washington was still working at a Philadelphia record wholesaler. "I was unloading boxes with my own name on them," Washington laughed, with a hint of irony.

Photo by Jeff Sedlik

Washington's soulful, sophisticated sound developed through the 1970s and the success of his next three albums—*All the Kings Horses, Soul Box,* and especially *Mister Magic*—landed him gigs as headliner in large concert halls and opened the door to session work with Bob James, Don Sebesky, Randy Weston, Eric Gale, Dave Grusin, and others. His success in the '70s continued with such albums as *Feels So Good, A Secret Place, Live at the Bijou, Reed Seed, Skylarkin',* and *Paradise.*

With the release of *Winelight* in 1980, Washington was finally recognized as one of the leading instrumental jazz masters. The album earned two Grammy awards for Best Jazz Fusion Recording and Best R & B Song, with Bill Withers, for "Just the Two of Us." *DownBeat* magazine crooned, "Washington plays with exquisite tone, range, and dexterity, grooving always." The *Boston Herald-American* proclaimed the album "A true masterpiece by an artist who has the ability to combine the better elements of pop, soul, and jazz and transform them into a form uniquely his."

In the early 80s, Washington played a major role in establishing the Philadelphia group Pieces of a Dream, for whom he produced three albums. Washington frequently performed the national anthem at Philadelphia 76ers games, revealing his lifelong passion for basketball. His musical prominence has taken him to the White House for President Clinton's first inauguration and to Radio City Music Hall to perform at President Clinton's 50th birthday celebration. Washington also performed the national anthem at the Special Olympics, and played a benefit concert for the Oklahoma City bombing victims.

Reflecting on his life, Washington said, "I'm thankful for the people who inspired me over the years: Dexter Gordon, Rahsaan Roland Kirk, Stanley Turrentine, Cannonball Adderley, Sonny Rollins, and Oliver Nelson. I would like to believe that some of the reasons I've been around so long is that I don't do the same thing over and over. I like to grow, keep adding another thread to my musical tapestry." He added, "I'm just staying true to the things that got me to play in the first place."

Washington died suddenly on December 17, 1999, shortly after taping a CBS-TV performance in New York. He was 56. His abbreviated career spanned 31 original and compilation albums, and many dozens of guest appearances on other artists' albums. His last major project was the March 2000 release of *Aria* on Sony Classical, an album of operatic arias by Puccini, Bizet, Massenet, and

Gershwin that took him back to his classical roots.

Washington always had hope for the future and left behind a remarkable humanitarian legacy as a public servant who was always willing to lend his name and talent to help others. "There is always hope; there is always optimism," he said. In order to preserve Washington's dream into the 21st century, The Grover Washington, Jr. Protect the Dream Foundation has been established. Its mission is to enrich the lives of young people through music education. The foundation recognizes the importance of music education and is committed to putting music back into the hands, minds, and hearts of every child possible. Tax-deductible contributions can be made to the Grover Washington Jr. Protect the Dream Foundation, 8610 Evergreen Place, Philadelphia, PA, 19118, with checks payable to GW Jr.—Protect the Dream.

Grover Washington, Jr., was a perennial. His music will withstand the test of charts, trends, and time. Washington's music was always about one thing, heart. It was the uncommon denominator that defined his life's work.

Photo by Jeff Sedlik

Photo by Jeff Sedlik

Contents

LEGEND

Special Symbols

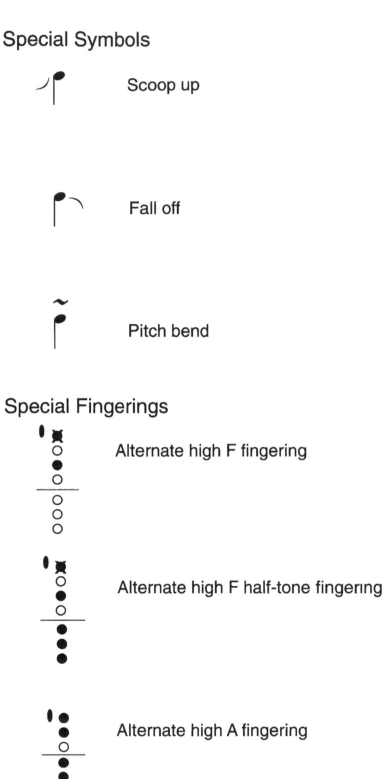

Scoop up

Fall off

Pitch bend

Special Fingerings

Alternate high F fingering

Alternate high F half-tone fingering

Alternate high A fingering

Chord Names

Note: Chord names in italics reflect actual sounding chords.
Chord names in regular type reflect chords respective to sax's written key.

In the Name of Love

Words and Music by Ralph MacDonald
and William Salter

Soprano Sax

Moderately bright

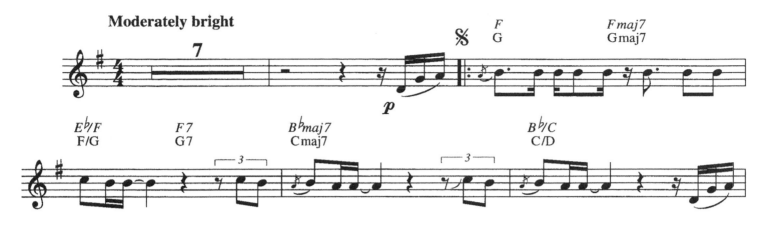

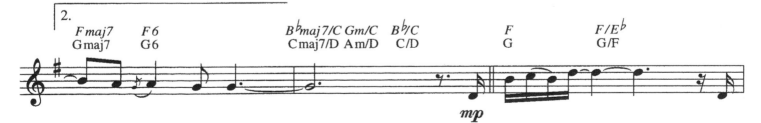

7

8

D.S. al Coda

Coda

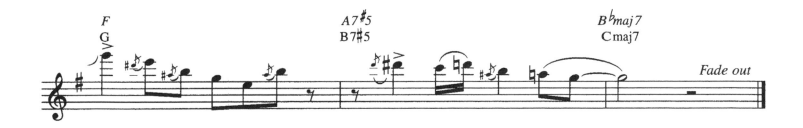

East River Drive

Written by Grover Washington, Jr.

Soprano Sax

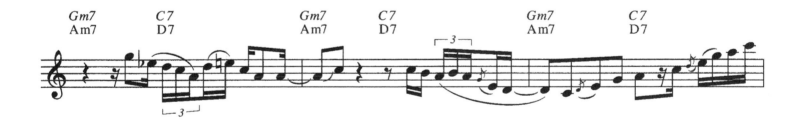

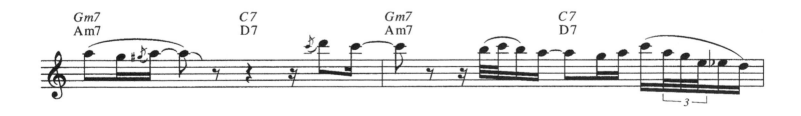

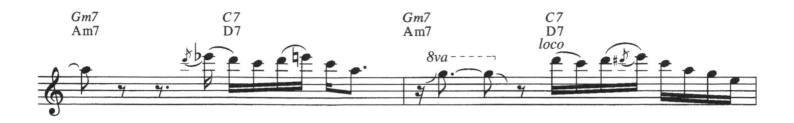

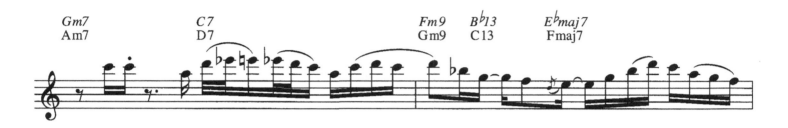

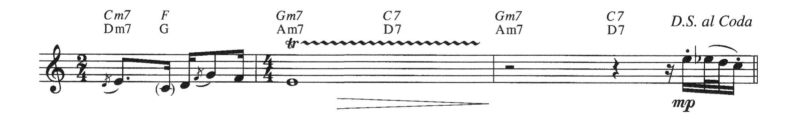

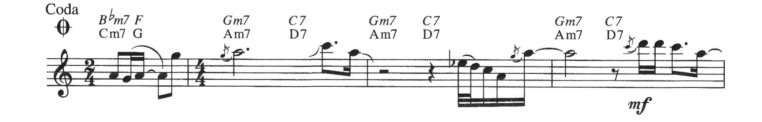

14

Begin fade

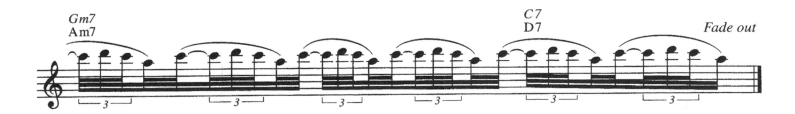

It Feels So Good

Words and Music by Ralph MacDonald
and William Salter

Tenor Sax

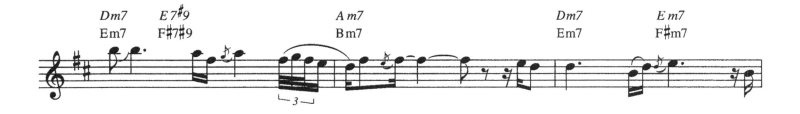

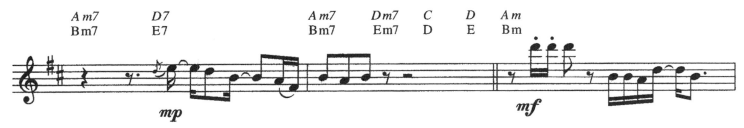

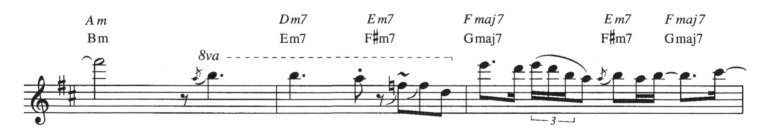

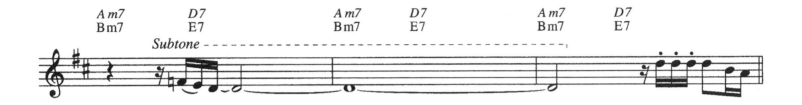

19

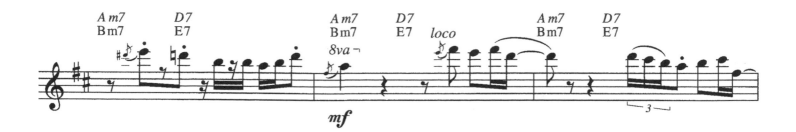

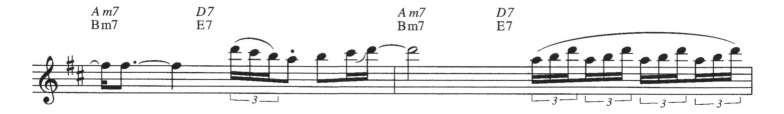

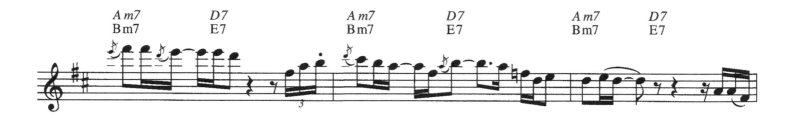

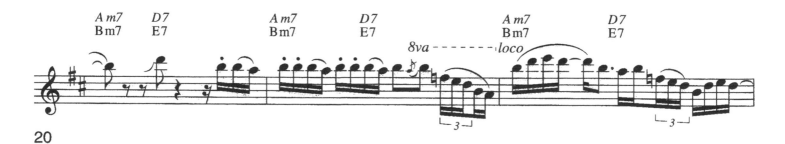

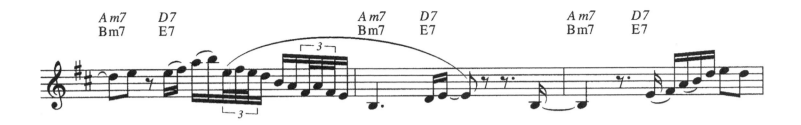

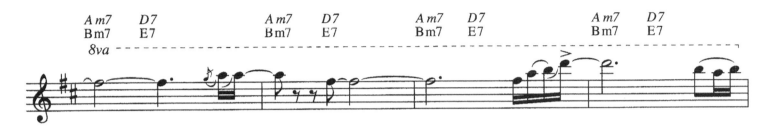

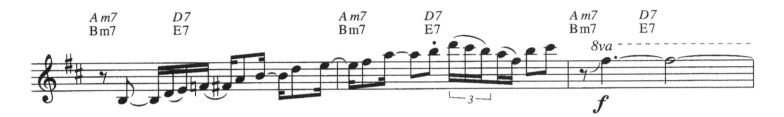

*Alternate high F fingering

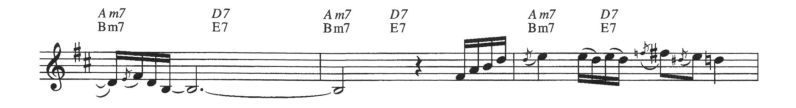

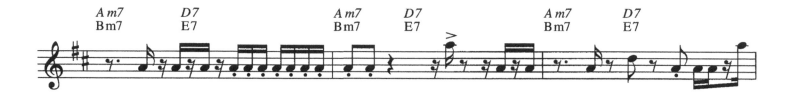

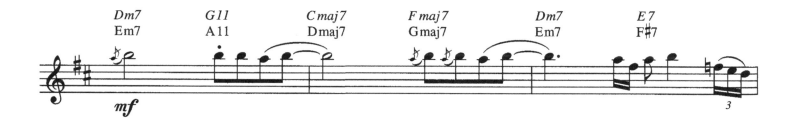

Just the Two of Us

Tenor Sax

Words and Music by Ralph MacDonald,
William Salter and Bill Withers

Moderately slow

Vocal (concert key)

I see the crys-tal rain-drops fall, and the beau-ty of it all is when the sun comes shin-ing
We look for love; no time for tears; wast-ed wa-ter's all that is and it don't make no flow-ers

through____ to make those rain-bows in my mind, when I think of you some-
grow.____ Good things might come to those who wait, not for those who wait too
dew.____ And dar-ling, when the morn-ing comes, and I see the morn-ing

I hear the crys-tal rain-drops fall on the win-dow down the hall and it be-comes the morn-ing

time, and I want to spend____ some time with you.____ Just____ the
late, and we've got to go____ for all we know.____
sun, I want to be____ the one with you.____

two of us, we can make it if____ we try;____ just the

two of us. (Just the two____ of us.) Just____ the two of us; { 1. 2. build-ing
3. build-ing

cas-tles in____ the sky;____ } just the two of us, you and I.____
cas-tles way____ up high;____

To Coda

24

Tenor Sax

* Alternate high F fingering
** Alternate high F half-tone fingering

25

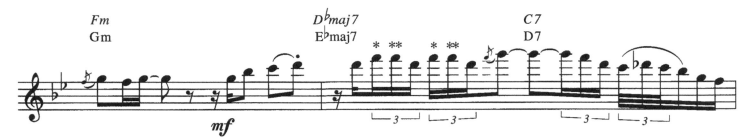

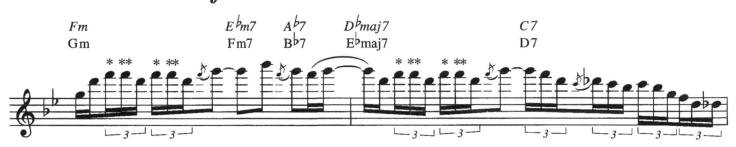

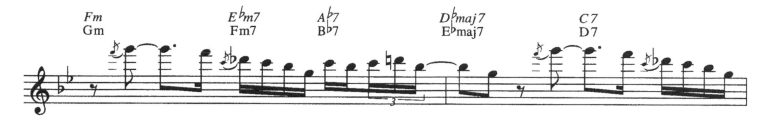

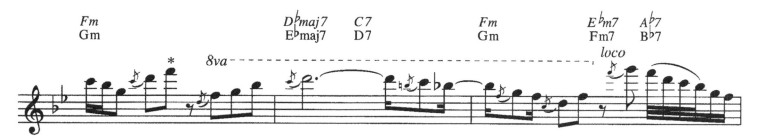

Coda   Tenor Sax

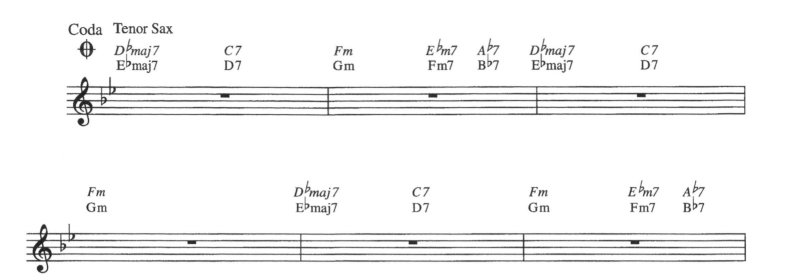

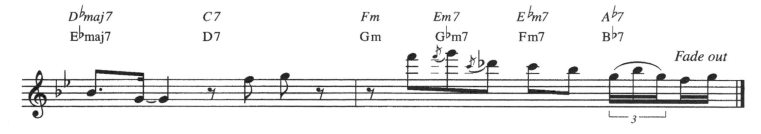

Let It Flow

Written by Grover Washington, Jr.

Alto Sax

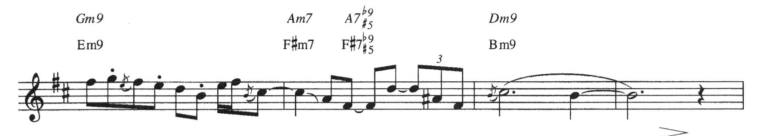

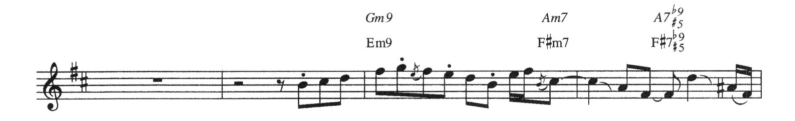

Dm
Bm

D7♭9   Gm9   Am7   A7♭9#5
B7♭9   Em9   F#m7   F#7♭9#5

Subtone -----

mp

Dm9
Bm9

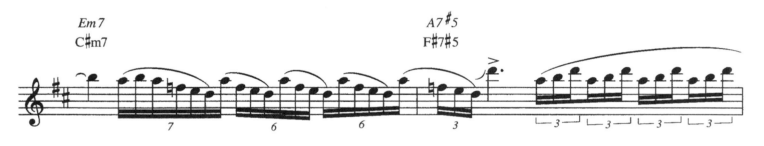

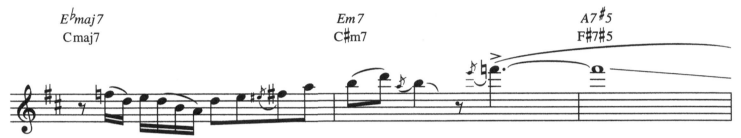

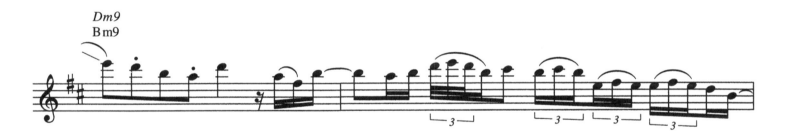

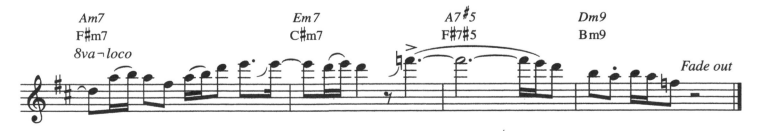

36

Mr. Magic

Words and Music by Ralph MacDonald
and William Salter

Tenor Sax

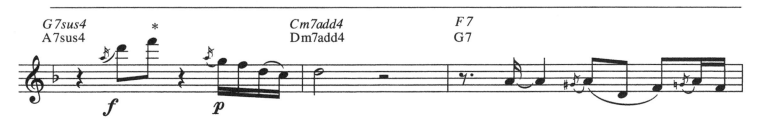

* Alternate high F fingering

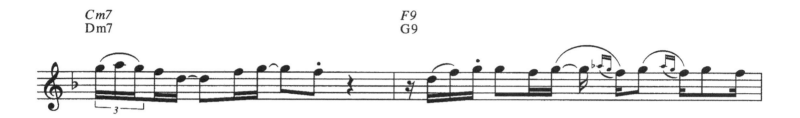

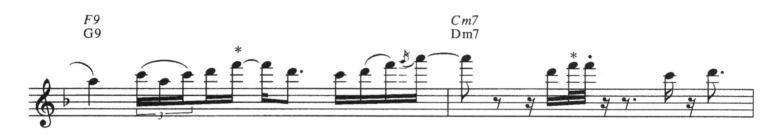

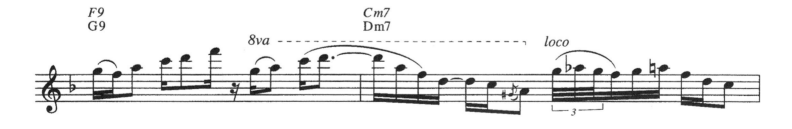

39

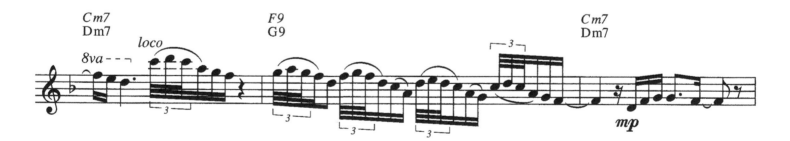

** Alternate high F half-tone fingering

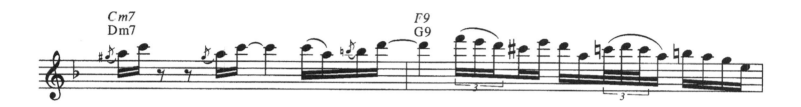

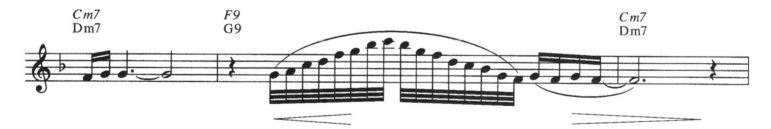

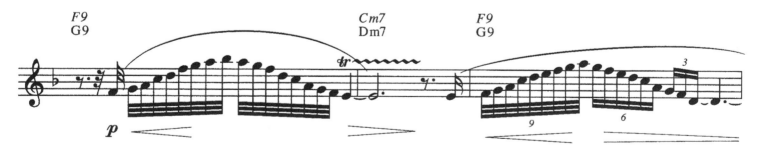

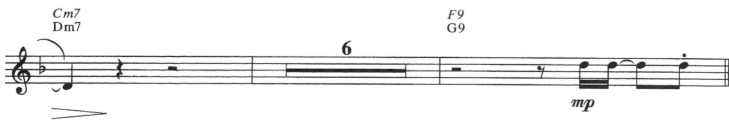

Begin fade

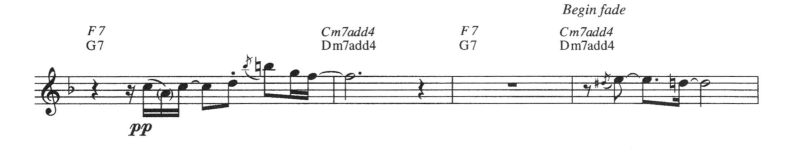

Fade out

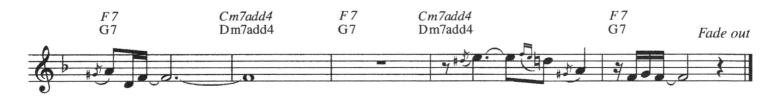

43

Little Black Samba

Words and Music by Ralph MacDonald,
William Salter and William Eaton

Tenor Sax

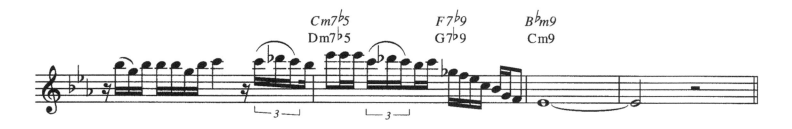

Vocal (concert)

I— know a—— place down— in old— South A - mer - i - ca,

right— there in— the heart— of Bra - zil, Ba - hi - a.—

That's— where peo - ple still— have strong— ties to Af - ri - ca,

and   their   mu - sic ech - oes the name Ni - ger - i - a.

Shan - go,   bı - che,   Ma - kum - ba,   all   tıed to - geth - er by

voo - doo,   mu - sıc. Peo - ple are   on a nat - 'ral hıgh.

Sam - ba   spır - ıt   ıs   a true   tes - ti - mo - nı - al

to   the   pow - er   of   Af - rı - ca's   rıt - u - al.

G♭maj7   F7♯9   Tacet

    Ev - 'ry nıght they sam - ba out   on the

G♭maj7   F7♯9   Tacet

beach - es.   It's a per - fect set - tıng for ro -

mance.   Let   your   bod - y   dance.————   It's   a   bac - cha - nal,————

————   with   a   feel - ing   just————   like   car - ni - val.————

Tenor Sax

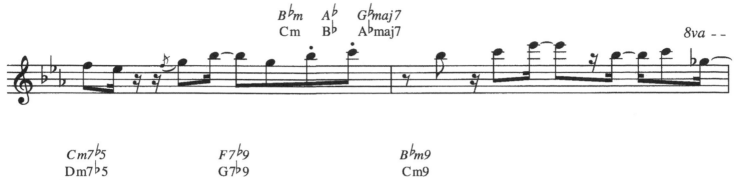

Vocal (concert)

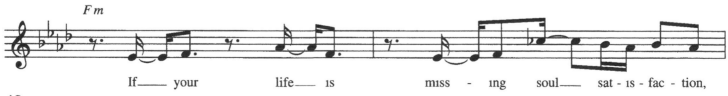

If___ your   life___ is   miss - ing soul___ sat - is - fac - tion,

re-mem - ber Ba - hia's wait - ing to just make___ it right.___

Ex - cite - ment, pas - sion, feel - ing all___ come to - geth - er in

mag - ic, fire___ burn - ing for you day___ or night.___

G♭maj7   F7#9   Tacet

___ Don't you know the sam - ba's wait - ing to

G♭maj7   F7#9   Tacet

get you?___ From the time you hear___ the mu - sic

E♭m9   ⌐3⌐   A♭13   A♭9#5   ⌐3⌐

start, it will take your heart,___ it will take your soul,___

D♭maj7   ⌐3⌐   Cm7♭5   F7♭9

___ it will take you if___ you're young___ or old.___

Tenor Sax

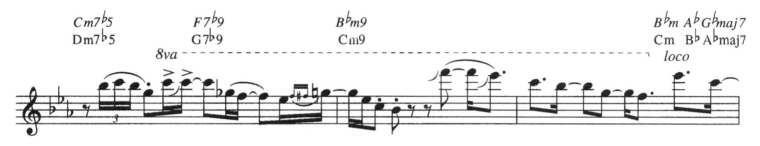

51

Make Me a Memory
(Sad Samba)

Alto Sax

Written by Grover Washington, Jr.

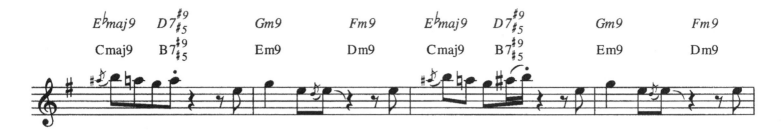

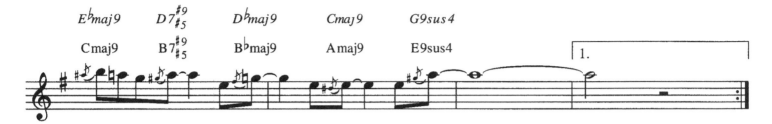

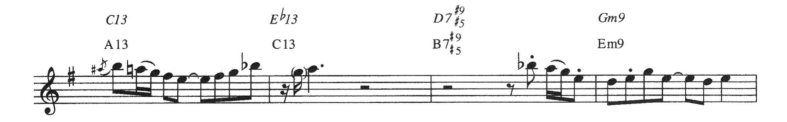

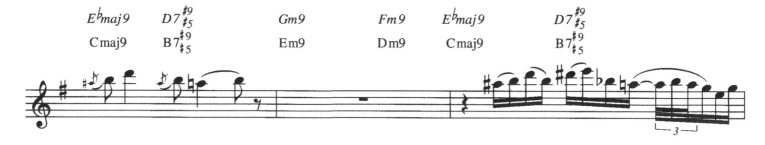

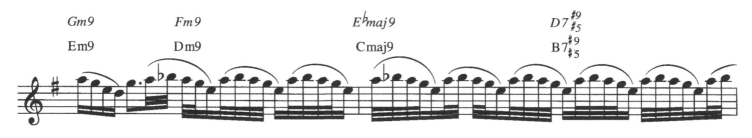

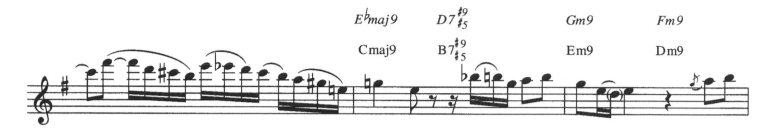

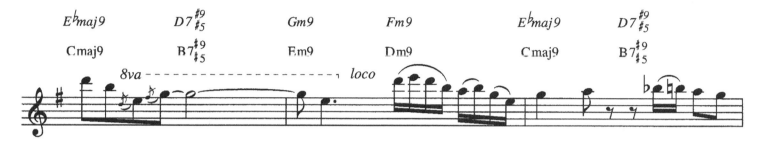

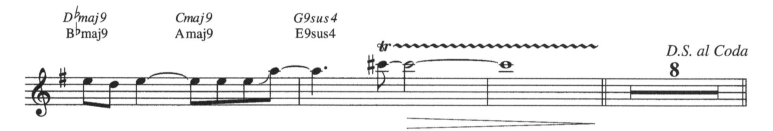

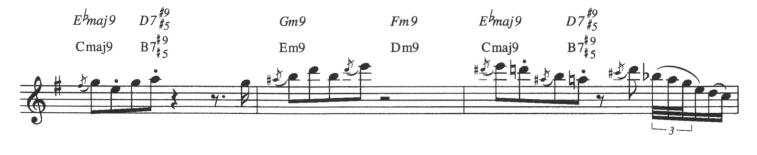

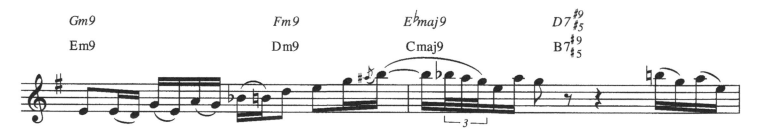

56

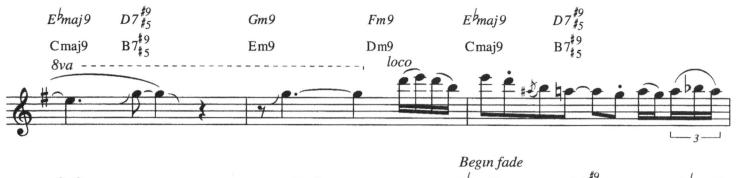

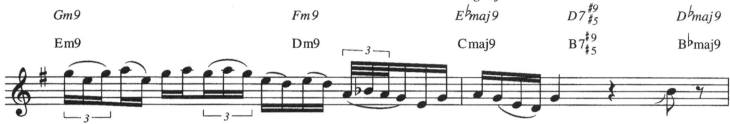

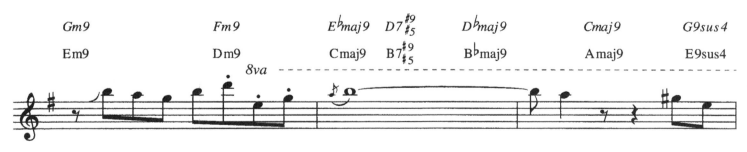

57

Passion Flower

Words by Milton Raskin
Music by Billy Strayhorn

Soprano Sax

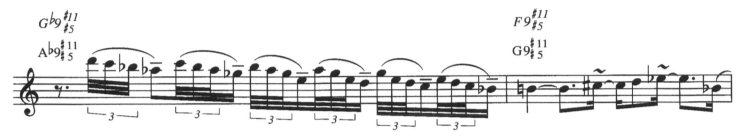

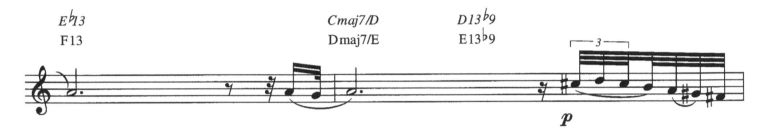

Take Five
(Another Take Five)

By Paul Desmond

Alto Sax

63

Am7 / E
F#m7/C#

C maj7　　　　　　　　*B m7*　　　　　　　　*A m7*
Amaj7　　　　　　　　 G#m7　　　　　　　　 F#m7

mf

Gmaj7　　　　　　　　　　　　　*C maj7*
Emaj7　　　　　　　　　　　　　 Amaj7

B m7　　　　　　　　*A m7*　　　　　　　　*B m7*
G#m7　　　　　　　　 F#m7　　　　　　　　 G#m7

Em11
C#m11

Percussion Solo

16

Em
C#m

mp

Em6
C#m6

Subtone - - - - - - - - - - - -

Em
C#m

Am7/E
F#m7/C#

C maj7
Amaj7

B m7
G#m7

A m7
F#m7

mf

Gmaj7
Emaj7

C maj7
Amaj7

B m7
G#m7

A m7
F#m7

B m7
G#m7

C maj7
Amaj7

B m7
G#m7

A m7
F#m7

Subtone - - - - - - - - - - - - -

Gmaj7
Emaj7

C maj7
Amaj7

B m7
G#m7

Begin fade

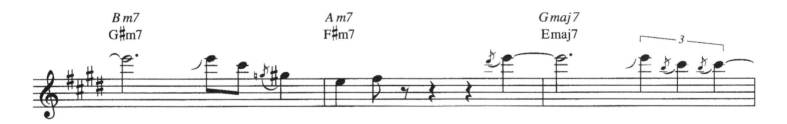

Fade out

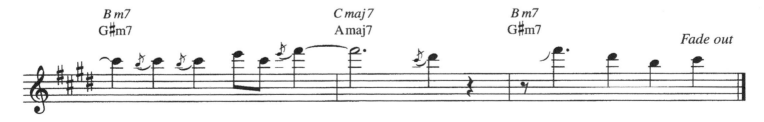

Take Me There

Written by Grover Washington, Jr.

* Alternate high F fingering
** Alternate high F half-tone fingering

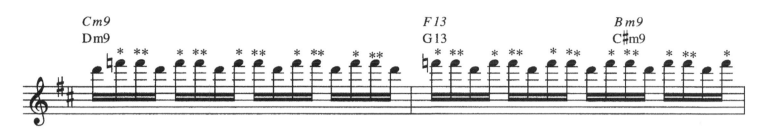

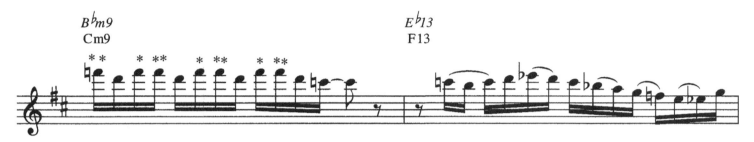

71

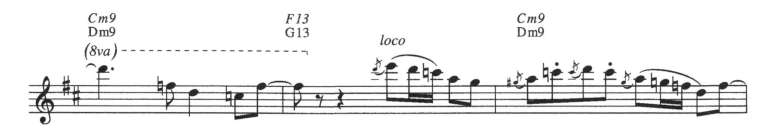

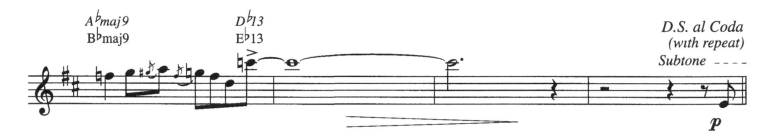

Time Out of Mind

Words and Music by Walter Becker
and Donald Fagen

To - night when I chase the drag - on, the wa -

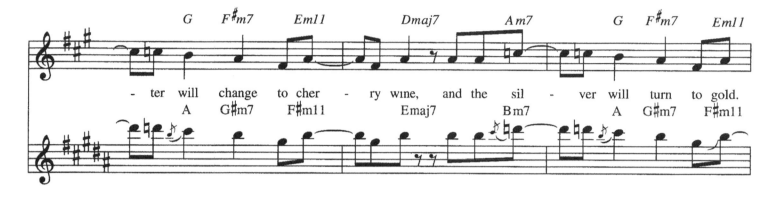

- ter will change to cher - ry wine, and the sil - ver will turn to gold.

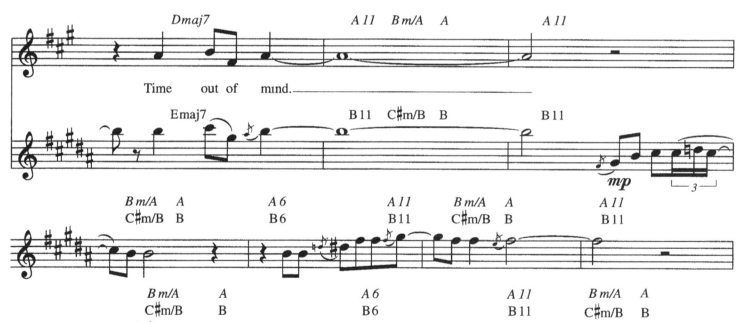

Time out of mind.

Vocal (concert)

Chil - dren, we have

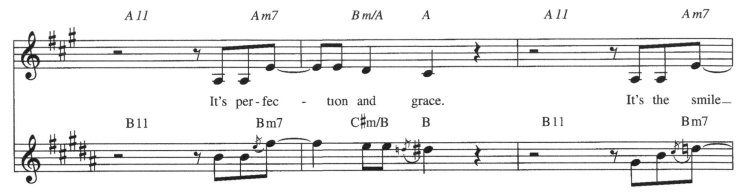

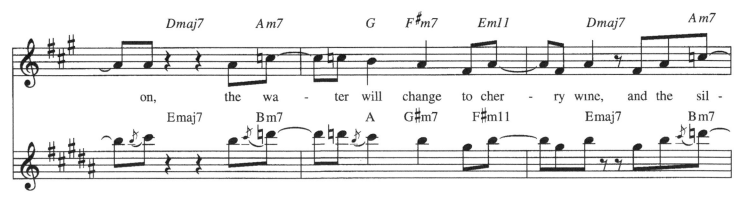

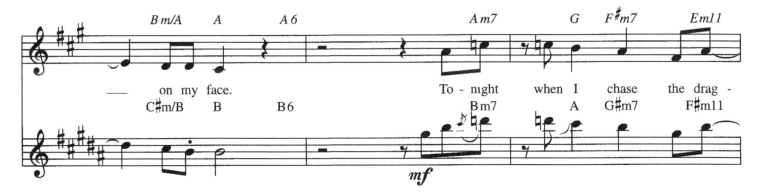

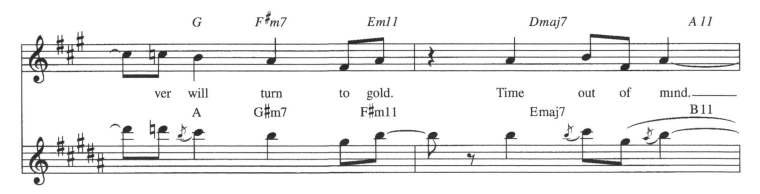

* Alternate high A fingering

Vocal (concert)

D.S. al Coda

Chil - dren, we have

Coda

78

* Alternate high A fingering

Winelight

Alto Sax

Words and Music by
William Eaton

Cm7
Am7

Cm7
Am7

Subtone -

mp

Subtone - - - - - - - -

8va - - - - - - -

loco

mf

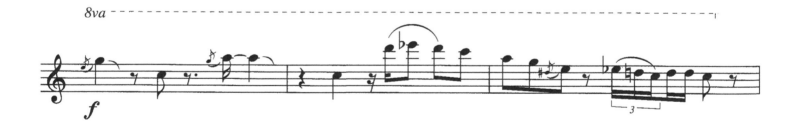

Coda

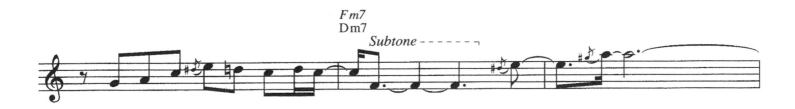

86

87

HAL•LEONARD® SAXOPHONE PLAY-ALONG

The Saxophone Play-Along Series will help you play your favorite songs quickly and easily. Just follow the music, listen to the audio to hear how the saxophone should sound, and then play along using the separate backing tracks. Each song is printed twice in the book: once for alto and once for tenor saxes. The online audio is available for streaming or download using the unique code printed inside the book, and it includes **PLAYBACK+** *options such as looping and tempo adjustments.*

1. ROCK 'N' ROLL
Bony Moronie • Charlie Brown • Hand Clappin' • Honky Tonk (Parts 1 & 2) • I'm Walkin' • Lucille (You Won't Do Your Daddy's Will) • See You Later, Alligator • Shake, Rattle and Roll.
00113137 Book/Online Audio $16.99

2. R&B
Cleo's Mood • I Got a Woman • Pick up the Pieces • Respect • Shot Gun • Soul Finger • Soul Serenade • Unchain My Heart.
00113177 Book/Online Audio $16.99

3. CLASSIC ROCK
Baker Street • Deacon Blues • The Heart of Rock and Roll • Jazzman • Smooth Operator • Turn the Page • Who Can It Be Now? • Young Americans.
00113429 Book/Online Audio $16.99

4. SAX CLASSICS
Boulevard of Broken Dreams • Harlem Nocturne • Night Train • Peter Gunn • The Pink Panther • St. Thomas • Tequila • Yakety Sax.
00114393 Book/Online Audio. $16.99

5. CHARLIE PARKER
Billie's Bounce (Bill's Bounce) • Confirmation • Dewey Square • Donna Lee • Now's the Time • Ornithology • Scrapple from the Apple • Yardbird Suite.
00118286 Book/Online Audio $16.99

6. DAVE KOZ
All I See Is You • Can't Let You Go (The Sha La Song) • Emily • Honey-Dipped • Know You by Heart • Put the Top Down • Together Again • You Make Me Smile.
00118292 Book/Online Audio $16.99

7. GROVER WASHINGTON, JR.
East River Drive • Just the Two of Us • Let It Flow • Make Me a Memory (Sad Samba) • Mr. Magic • Take Five • Take Me There • Winelight.
00118293 Book/Online Audio $16.99

8. DAVID SANBORN
Anything You Want • Bang Bang • Chicago Song • Comin' Home Baby • The Dream • Hideaway • Slam • Straight to the Heart.
00125694 Book/Online Audio $16.99

9. CHRISTMAS
The Christmas Song (Chestnuts Roasting on an Open Fire) • Christmas Time Is Here • Count Your Blessings Instead of Sheep • Do You Hear What I Hear • Have Yourself a Merry Little Christmas • The Little Drummer Boy • White Christmas • Winter Wonderland.
00148170 Book/Online Audio $16.99

10. JOHN COLTRANE
Blue Train (Blue Trane) • Body and Soul • Central Park West • Cousin Mary • Giant Steps • Like Sonny (Simple Like) • My Favorite Things • Naima (Niema).
00193333 Book/Online Audio $16.99

11. JAZZ ICONS
Body and Soul • Con Alma • Oleo • Speak No Evil • Take Five • There Will Never Be Another You • Tune Up • Work Song.
00199296 Book/Online Audio $16.99

12. SMOOTH JAZZ
Bermuda Nights • Blue Water • Europa • Flirt • Love Is on the Way • Maputo • Songbird • Winelight.
00248670 Book/Online Audio $16.99

13. BONEY JAMES
Butter • Let It Go • Stone Groove • Stop, Look, Listen (To Your Heart) • Sweet Thing • Tick Tock • Total Experience • Vinyl.
00257186 Book/Online Audio $16.99